BEYOND BELIEF

Thanks for being such an unbelievable boss.
You are very special. Barbara

BEYOND BELIEF

Cartoon Confessions of Faith by Roger Judd

Foreword by Kevin Frank

CORNERSTONE PRESS CHICAGO
CHICAGO, ILLINOIS

Published by Cornerstone Press Chicago, the publishing arm of Jesus People USA Covenant Church. Jesus People USA is a community of Christians serving the poor, the homeless, and the elderly in the Uptown neighborhood of Chicago. On a national and international level, Jesus People is known for Cornerstone *magazine, the bands on the Grrr* recordS *label (REZ, Cauzin' efekt, CRASHDOG, and the Crossing), and for Cornerstone Festival. If you would like more information about Jesus People USA and its outreaches, write JPUSA care of Cornerstone Press Chicago, 939 W. Wilson Ave., Chicago, IL 60640.*

ISBN 0-940895-26-9
Printed in the United States of America.
97   96   95   94   4   3   2   1

Cover design by Pat Peterson, illustration by Roger Judd.

Library of Congress Cataloging-in Publication Data

Judd,   Roger,   1950–
    Beyond belief : cartoon confessions of faith / Roger Judd ;   foreword by Kevin Frank.
        p.   cm.
    ISBN 0-940895-26-9
    1. Christian life--Caricatures and cartoons.   2. American wit and humor, Pictorial.   I. Title.
BV4517.J85   1994
202'.07--dc20   94-25012
                                                                                                      CIP

To Jill.
Thanks for your love, your support,
and for all the times you've
made me laugh.

Foreword

People like to read comic strips because they transcend the barriers of race, age, and gender to deliver a quick, easy laugh. An investment of three or four seconds will be recouped by a smile that lasts all day. What few people realize is just how disarming a comic can be. You catch yourself belly laughing at a political strip that you disagree with, simply because it's drawn funny. Little do you suspect that your carefully guarded opinion has been ever-so-slightly influenced. Maybe that other guy isn't so very wrong after all.

Beyond Belief is an excellent example of a comic strip at its best. Roger Judd's distinctive, reader-friendly style is so masterfully rendered that you can't help but stop and look. His clean line art conveys complex situations and emotions in a loose, flowing pen stroke that makes it look like it was easy. The characters he creates are a magical blend of satire and sympathy. We're not sure if we're laughing at them, or at ourselves.

But it's the punch line that gets you. Roger avoids the cheap clichés to forge real truth beneath the laughs. Long after the grin has faded, you'll find yourself with a sliver of conviction wedged firmly between the cerebellum and cerebrum. Take for instance the strip about a guy praying that it's not *his* house on fire. I've done that, so I burst out in guffaws. It's only later that I start to think it over and find myself challenged. Or encouraged. Or enlightened. Or uplifted. Mr. Judd cuts a wide swath when he pulls that pen out of the scabbard.

The strips in this collection are as good as any you'll find in the daily papers, and better than most. They deal with situations that are common to us all. From weariness to joy, from the politically correct to the theologically misguided, *Beyond Belief* sheds light on it all. I won't be surprised to see the day come when I find Roger's work staring out at me from the morning newspaper. In fact, I look forward to that day.

It gives me great pleasure to introduce you to Roger Judd and *Beyond Belief.* You can thank me later.

KEVIN FRANK
Creator of Oboe Jones

SURE I LIKE IT HERE. IT'S FANTASTIC, IT'S HEAVEN. WHAT'S NOT TO LIKE?

BUT YES I AM JUST A LITTLE IRRITATED, KNOWING THAT WE COULD HAVE BEEN HERE THREE YEARS AGO...

... HAD IT NOT BEEN FOR THAT OAT BRAN DIET YOU PUT US THROUGH.

EXAMINE YOUR PRAYERS — CASE # 43:

WHEN A FIRETRUCK PASSES YOU, HEADING TOWARDS YOUR NEIGHBORHOOD, DO YOU...

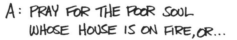

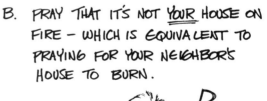

A: PRAY FOR THE POOR SOUL WHOSE HOUSE IS ON FIRE, OR...

RRRRRR

B. PRAY THAT IT'S NOT YOUR HOUSE ON FIRE — WHICH IS EQUIVALENT TO PRAYING FOR YOUR NEIGHBOR'S HOUSE TO BURN.

RRRRRR

IT WAS THE LITTLE KNOWN DISCIPLE WAYNE WHO FIRST TRIED TO INTRODUCE PUPPETS INTO THE MINISTRY.

parsonage

par·son·age (pär's'n ij)
n. [ME. *personage* < OFr. < ML. (Ec)
personagium, THE DWELLING
PROVIDED BY THE CHURCH
WHERE THE PARSON AGES.